THE LITTLE BOOK of

DO!

ACT ON YOUR PA
FOR A LIFE OF SUC

KEL LANDIS III

ISBN 978-1505318746

Books are available for special promotions. For
details, contact:

Somnium Factorem LLC
2710 Rosedale Avenue
Raleigh, NC 27607

e-mail: sales@SomniumFactorem.com

Edited by David B. Magee
Book design by Paul Fitzgerald

Printed in the United States of America

DEDICATION

This book is dedicated to my mom (Corinne) and my dad (Big Kel) who always believed in me. They exemplified the lessons and themes described in this book.

To my two wonderful children, Dorsey and "HK," for whom I would do anything. As they create their lives, I learn much by simply observing.

Finally, to my best friend and wife, Nina. Her boundless energy reflects a life of *do* more than anyone I know, while her passion for doing good and making a difference inspire me daily.

TABLE *of* CONTENTS

PREFACE

A few years after college, graduate school, and working in other cities, I returned to my hometown of Rocky Mount, North Carolina, where I had the privilege of serving as president of the local Chamber of Commerce. It was particularly meaningful given that my father had held the same post two decades earlier. When I eventually passed the gavel to my successor, I received a framed print with a quote (most often) attributed to John Wesley. Ultimately, this quote was the inspiration for the title *The Little Book of Do!* It read:

DO

all the good you can...by all the means you can...in all the ways you can, in all the places you can, for all the people you can…as long as ever you can.

Like others, I have my deficiencies and shortcomings. But initiative is not among them. I am (or at least I have *become*) a "doer." It's an inextricable part of who I am, and it defines how I live. I've been fortunate. I've enjoyed a successful career in banking, investments, and private equity; I've served on the boards of a variety of worthy non-profits; and I've been an involved community leader—at all levels—particularly in education and economic development. In each of these experiences, *do* was the difference maker in what I was able to contribute and accomplish. Moreover, it's been the key driver of whatever success I've achieved as a businessperson, entrepreneur, and (more importantly) as an action-oriented contributor to mycommunity.

I've observed that successful and happy people have one thing in common—they are doers. They pursue and do those things that stir their passions. As a result, they are enthusiastic, persistent, and exhibit a can-do attitude.

Of course, I'm neither the first nor the only one to

discover the power of *do*. Teacher, author, and lecturer Marianne Williamson understands it, and she reflects it in one of my favorite quotes taken from her book *A Return to Love*. She writes:

> Our deepest fear is not that we are inadequate. Our deepest fear is that we are powerful beyond measure. It is our light, not our darkness that most frightens us. We ask ourselves, "Who am I to be brilliant, gorgeous, talented, fabulous?" Actually, who are you not to be? You are a child of God. Your playing small does not serve the world. There is nothing enlightened about shrinking so that other people won't feel insecure around you. We are all meant to shine, as children do. We were born to make manifest the glory of God that is within us. It's not just in some of us; it's in everyone. And as we let our own light shine, we unconsciously give other people permission to do the same. As we are liberated from our own fear, our

presence automatically liberates others.

It's my conviction that if we each had the courage and motivation to prioritize our pursuits and act on our passions— the essence of *do*—we would all benefit, both individually and collectively.

Convinced by my own experiences and having witnessed the power of do in others, I was compelled to share what I've learned in this book. And as I studied and researched this phenomenon, I discovered countless examples of how do changed lives and changed history. In the chapters that follow, we'll explore the liberating and exhilarating power of do, and how your doing will inspire others to do the same. My hope is that you find plenty of practical and actionable nuggets in the message.

INTRODUCTION

Just do it.

We've all seen the Nike slogan emblazoned on shirts, bags, and billboards. But, chances are you've never really thought much about it. Yet, when understood, embraced, and incorporated into the way we live, the notion of doing (as opposed to hoping, thinking about doing, or making excuses for not doing) becomes a catalyst for success in all aspects of life.

Do is no New Age fad. If anything, *do* is a set of learned skills with the power to energize the life of anyone with the courage to employ it. By analogy, *do* isn't a new mode of transportation but a potent fuel additive—one that can transform a sputtering, oil- burning gas-guzzler into a powerful and efficient doing machine.

Best of all, *do* doesn't require a course or seminar to understand. Neither will you spend years pursuing it before you feel and reap the benefits. In this one little book, you have all you need to become a doer.

So let's get doing!

ACKNOWLEDGEMENTS

David Magee is an intelligent, creative man. When I described my vision for this book, he got it immediately. As I put thoughts to paper, he organized my concepts and improved upon my words. His contributions to this book were invaluable.

CHAPTER ONE
Do Now

"You may delay, but time will not."
— Ben Franklin

Time is our most precious and fleeting commodity. Once passed, it can't be recovered with any amount of money or effort.

The average 30-year-old has 18,927 days to make something of his or her life. The average 45-year-old has roughly 14,000, while 60-year-olds have but 9000. Don't let these cold numbers depress you. Instead, let them motivate you to make the best and most of each day.

Whether whispered to ourselves or said to others, we all

have things we dream of doing. They're the fill-in-the-blank pursuits that follow the preface, "One day I'm going to …"

Frequently, but not always, these wanna-do's reflect deeply held desires and passions. Even so, we allow months, years, and even lifetimes to pass with no meaningful progress. Invariably, we make excuses as to why now is not the time then kick our dreams down the road, yet again.

Wanna-do's come in all shapes and sizes. Some are smaller than others, like beginning an exercise program, volunteering time to a community project, or changing an unhealthy habit. Others are more substantial, such as pursuing a new career, running for public office, or relocating to a place you've always wanted to live. Irrespective, they all have one thing in common: none will ever be accomplished without action— doing something about it.

When we set and achieve a lofty goal, we feel good. But the good feelings usually kick in long before we actually cross the finish line. In truth, just taking action—any action—in pursuit of a deeply held passion can be transformative.

Conversely, when we kick our dreams down the road and put off doing what we really need or desire to do, the opposite occurs. We beat ourselves up for lacking courage and initiative. We might even externalize it and blame others for our inaction. Over time, these feelings erode our confidence and sense of worth. We feel paralyzed, powerless, and resentful. But, it doesn't have to be that way.

We have the power to change both ourselves and (in most cases) our circumstances. The transformation begins the instant we take the initiative. That's our *do* moment and, if we think about our own experience, we know this to be true.

We've all had spells, for example, during which we couldn't muster the motivation to exercise. Our excuses are vast and varied, but the end result is always the same—we feel unhealthy, lethargic, and, most of all, guilty. Not surprising, our self-confidence plunges. Yet, how quickly those negative thoughts and emotions dissipate when we finally drag ourselves up and go on a brisk walk or run, or go to the pool or gym. One workout and we're back in the saddle! We're back in control. Our self-confidence surges.

In this book, we'll examine the reasons we don't do what we really want to do. We'll extol the virtues and benefits of action and explain why doing or not doing is a question of individual choice. With just a little understanding, encouragement, and direction, you too can become a doer. In return, you'll be happier, healthier, and enjoy, a more satisfying life. In the process, you'll even make the world around you a better place for others.

It's often said, "There's no time like the present." It's trite, but true. Life is short and fleeting. The time to act on things you deem important is now.

Takeaway:

Do what matters ... NOW!

CHAPTER TWO
What to Do?

*"Desires dictate our priorities, priorities shape our choices,
and choices determine our actions."*
— Dallin H. Oaks

For each of our wanna-do's, there are a dozen must-do's and ought-to-do's clamoring for our time and attention. They clutter our heads, pull us in multiple directions, and leave us exhausted and overextended. Sometimes the best we can do is simply get through the day. That's surviving, not living.

Do is not meant to imply that we should act on every passionate impulse. That would be unrealistic, irresponsible, and potentially hazardous. Instead, we need a rational process for vetting competing pursuits. We need a practical methodology for deciding which pursuits to delay, which to dismiss, and which to pursue as if our lives depended on it.

I once heard a pastor deliver a speech at the inauguration of a new president for a notable university in Virginia. (Though a pastor, he also served on the board of a *Fortune* 100 company.) One statement in particular stuck with me. He said that every new initiative must begin with an "honest existential assessment of context."

An honest existential assessment of context?

On its face, that sounds like a mouthful. Yet, one doesn't need to be versed in existentialism or have knowledge of Kierkegaard or Sartre to understand its meaning. Simply put, we must evaluate our pursuits openly and honestly in the context of the world around us. We must understand how they affect us personally.

On a daily basis, we make decisions that affect how and where we expend time and energy. Usually they appear in the form of tasks, opportunities, and obligations. *What should we do? What should we not do? Which take priority?*

These questions are more easily answered if we evaluate and filter our pursuits using three simple criteria:

1. Importance
2. Passion
3. Urgency

IMPORTANCE

What's important to me may not be important to you. It's subjective, and each of us must decide individually. Still, when facing tough calls on importance, you might ask yourself these questions:

- Is the activity really significant?

- Is it of great value to me personally or professionally?

- Will doing it or not doing it influence my success?

- Will it affect my survival or well-being?

- How will my decision affect co-workers, friends, or family members?

- Sometimes the importance of a given matter is driven by the personal relationships involved. A middle school soccer game, for example, may not sound important.

But when it's your child on the field, it can be more important than a business meeting.

After weighing the importance of a given pursuit, consider ascribing a personal importance rating of, say, one to five with one being "not important" and five being "very important."

PASSION

Next, consider your passion for the contemplated pursuit. I do it by visualizing myself seated before a device with wires and pads like an EKG. Only this (fictitious) contraption is a passion meter. When hypothetically affixed to the heart and head, it measures the subject's passion with a reading of one to five. If the contemplated pursuit doesn't move the needle to at least a four, then we should probably decline (that is unless it deserves a high "importance" rating).

When facing tough calls on passion, ask yourself these questions:

- How will this pursuit make me feel?

- Am I inspired enough to complete the task or pursuit?

- Does it affect my happiness?

For most of my life, I was a runner, and some 25 years ago I set my sights on running a marathon. Specifically, I wanted to run the New York Marathon. This was long before the current marathon craze and, at the time, it was a lofty ambition.

My passion meter was high, and I trained hard. Weekdays, I ran four to 10 miles per day. On weekends, I ran further, starting at 10 miles and eventually progressing to 24. One Sunday morning, I ran 21 miles and even managed to be home in time to pull a volunteer shift in the church nursery.

After six months of training, I ran the New York Marathon and I finished in a respectable time. By then, however, my goal had changed: I wanted to run the big one, the Boston Marathon.

Running "Boston" isn't as easy as registering and showing up. One must qualify, and my New York time did not. So, I ran the New York Marathon again. Though I did markedly better, it still wasn't good enough for a ticket to

Boston.

My next chance to qualify was the Marine Corps Marathon in Washington, D.C. There I ran the first 23 miles faster than ever, but at mile 24, my legs locked up like pillars of granite. I staggered across the finish line four minutes shy of a qualifying time; I was devastated.

Still passionate and unwilling to throw in the towel, I began searching for other marathons in the area. I found one in Greensboro, North Carolina, three weeks later. Still recovering from the physical trauma of the Marine Corps Marathon, I ran my best time ever. With a 3:07 time, I qualified for Boston!

Five months after Greensboro, I turned onto Boylston Street in downtown Boston amidst tens of thousands of excited onlookers. Three-and-a-half blocks later, I finished the Boston Marathon with a respectable time. I had set my sights on something big (for me), and employing all the passion, discipline, and perseverance I could muster, I had achieved it.

Reflecting back, I'm immensely grateful for the experience. I also know that it could never have happened but for a truckload of passion (and dogged determination). How else does one find the motivation to roll out of bed at 5 a.m. on an otherwise lazy Sunday morning and run 20 miles?

Sometimes when we take on a big personal challenge, our goals and ambitions grow during the pursuit. We don't always know where these new endeavors will take us. But often we end up doing something that's bigger than we could have imagined. Do inspired me to dream big (but realistically), then sustained me until I had achieved my evolving objectives. As they grew, I grew.

I liken passions to sandbars along a river: they shift and change with time. During the years following my marathon experiences, I developed severe back problems that required multiple surgeries. As a result, I had to give up my greatest passion: running. Even so, I've found satisfaction in walking. I do a fast three-mile walk on weekdays and a seven-miler on weekends. It isn't the same as running, but the physical and mental release of being outside and exercising still moves my passion meter enough to get me up and out outside almost every day—"weather or not."

URGENCY

Urgency is a third consideration when filtering tasks, pursuits, and obligations that occupy our time. It relates to the need for swift action, and for most pursuits, it's an easy evaluation. For those that aren't so clear-cut, here are a few questions you might ask yourself:

- Is this an activity that can only be done by a certain date lest the opportunity disappear? In other words, is the train leaving the station?

- Does the action have a firm deadline to which you've previously agreed?

- What effect would a delay have on others?

- Is it an emergency? ... a REAL emergency?

Certain items should circumvent evaluation and go straight to the top of our priority list. Seeing the physician for a serious (or potentially serious) problem is a good example. Another— at least from my perspective—relates to business commitments. If I make a commitment to deliver a project by a specified date, I'm all-hands-on-deck until delivery is complete.

PULLING IT TOGETHER AND RECONCILING WHAT TO DO

Stephen Covey offered a two-dimensional matrix of urgency versus importance combinations in his book *First Things First* (Free Press, 1994). Kicking it up a notch, I've created a 3D matrix. I call it the Do Wedge©, and it depicts various combinations of importance, passion, and urgency. In essence, it's a visual framework for categorizing and prioritizing the many pursuits that compete for our time and energy.

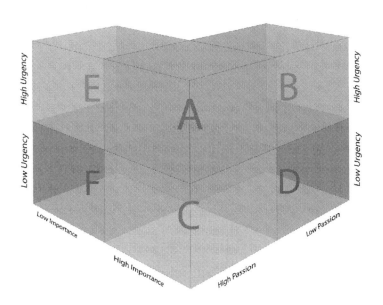

LOOKING AT EACH QUADRANT INDIVIDUALLY

A	☑ High Importance
	☑ High Passion
	☑ High Urgency

If there's a sweet spot in the Do Wedge©, this is it. These activities go directly to the top of our to-do list. For me, walking daily is a good example. Besides the   obvious physical and mental benefits of routine exercise (both high importance items), I love being outdoors (a high passion item).

Relish pursuits in this quadrant, and, as much as possible, fill your life with *do* activities that are both important and earn high, passion ratings.

B	☑ High Importance
	☐ High Passion
	☑ High Urgency

We all must do things that are important and urgent but not much fun. Finishing our taxes to make a filing deadline is a good example. For me, I love walking but loathe weight training (though I know it's important to good health as I age). Consequently, I have to make myself do it.

Because there's no passion involved, we may need to reach deep to find the motivation for pursuits in this category. But they're still high-priority activities. Do these now and without hesitation. Afterward, scratch them off your list and pat yourself on the back for getting them done.

C	☑ High Importance
	☑ High Passion
	☐ High Urgency

Here, the task is important and it moves our passion meter, but there is no pressing deadline to dictate timing. The question isn't whether we do them, but when.

A do activity that belongs in this quadrant (but is often overlooked) is think time or planning time for life—personal and professional. These are important do activities, and while they may not have to be done today or tomorrow, strategic thinking should be somewhere on our to-do list.

D	☑ High Importance
	☐ High Passion
	☐ High Urgency

Because these items have high importance, they do need to get done. Again, the question is when? Having a discussion with a co-worker about team effectiveness is a possible example.

It's easy to procrastinate (or outright avoid) items in this category. But, resist the urge and find the time before the deadline or window of opportunity passes.

Having passions and pursuing those passions is essential to personal fulfillment. They produce great joy and

E	☐ High Importance ☑ High Passion ☑ High Urgency

satisfaction and, consequently, they're critical elements of do.

So, let's not push this category of pursuits so far down the list of priorities that we never get to them.

The only difference between these pursuits and those in

F	☐ High Importance ☑ High Passion ☐ High Urgency

Category E is urgency. For the same reasons given supra, let's not forgo pursuits about which we are deeply passionate. Instead, let's just make them lower priority items then get to them as time permits. Playing golf is a good example. In the scheme of things, it isn't exactly important (unless it's your livelihood). But, if it creates joy, you should find time to do it.

G	☐ High Importance ☐ High Passion ☐ High Urgency

Don't waste your time. Take a pass on these opportunities, and reallocate your time to higher priority pursuits.

ABOUT SAYING "NO"

We can create and incorporate an intelligent system for

prioritizing and filtering the things that usurp our time, but if we lack the ability to say "no" when appropriate, we've accomplished little to nothing. We'll continue to clog our system with low- importance, low-passion, low-urgency pursuits.

Each day we're asked to do things. If these requests involve (or will involve) material expenditures of time and energy, we should evaluate them on the basis of importance, passion, and urgency.

Personally, I have plenty of room for improvement when it comes to saying "no." It's a weakness that doesn't serve me well. If someone asks me to do something that excites me, my tendency is to respond with a quick "yes" without evaluating the request relative to other priorities. Nevertheless, developing an ability to say "no" is important, and here are some useful tidbits that have helped me along the way:

- When you know in your toes that the request is not important, not urgent, or doesn't inspire you, respond with a quick and polite "no."

- If uncertain, ask the person making the request if you can have time to think it over. Time removes us from the heat of the moment and allows us to put the request in perspective. If, upon reflection, you decide that it doesn't meet your do criteria, you'll find it easier to say "no" and your basis for declining will be easier to explain.

- If you judge the request to be important but you don't believe you can do it within the time allotted, consider a modified "yes" such as, "Yes, I can help but I can only do it this way." Then proceed to explain the way you propose to help. Alternatively, you might consider a qualified no such as, "No, I can't do it. But I can do something else for you." Then explain what you can do.

I've said, I haven't yet perfected the art of saying "no." But just being aware of my own impulsive tendencies is beneficial and a big step toward improvement. I'm far more likely to pause, evaluate the pursuit, and make better decisions today than I may have done in the past.

ACHIEVABILITY

Finally, before allocating significant time to a new pursuit or goal, assess whether the objective is actually achievable. Words like "difficult" or "improbable" shouldn't necessarily dissuade one from going forward. But truly "impossible" is a different matter altogether. Vowing to swim the English Channel is one thing. Aiming to swim from California to Hawaii, however, is impossible. Don't set yourself up for failure. That benefits no one.

As you formulate your list of things you wish to accomplish, keep the difficult items but leave out the impossibilities. Each should be achievable given realistic time and resource constraints. If this is the wrong time in life or the wrong time given other priorities, postpone execution for a better time—whether that's next month or next year.

Deciding what is and what isn't actually achievable isn't always easy. Most of these assessments will be made based on simple reasoning and gut feel. Ask yourself:

- Can I achieve this with hard work and determination alone?

- Do I have the resources I need to achieve this goal or initiative?

- Do I have the requisite support, money, or assistance I need from others?

At the end of the day, we must consider the information at our disposal and make a decision as to whether the objective is within the zone of possibility. But, be careful not to allow examination to become another excuse for not doing. It's called "paralysis by analysis," and we're all susceptible. The key is to know when you've examined enough.

Patrick Lencioni, in his book The Five Temptations of a CEO, discusses the inclination of many CEOs to obtain 100% certainty with respect to a given issue before making a decision. While there's nothing wrong with total certainty, it's rarely achievable and it takes too long to get there. A better standard, writes Lencioni, is to seek 80% "clarity" in a reasonable amount of time, then decide and act.

DEEP GUT EXCEPTION

There are do actions that can only be described as deeply felt calls to action that don't easily fit into any of the Do Wedge© quadrants. These are deep gut feelings that compel us to action, and it's the essence of a phrase we've all heard, "A man's gotta do what a man's gotta do."

I came across this "man's gotta do" quote in a restaurant

while writing this book. It was the caption on a framed photo of John Wayne. Although, interestingly enough, John Wayne didn't actually recite this in any of his movies, he did come close. In Stagecoach, he said, "Well, there's some things a man just can't run away from," and in Hondo he said, "A man oughta do what he thinks is best." The closest "gotta do" quote actually came from John Steinbeck's The Grapes of Wrath: "a man got to do what he got to do."

Despite who said it first or best, this simple statement reflects a category of do that doesn't fit neatly into any time-management matrix. Instead, these do items are driven by powerful feelings of duty, calling, and crisis that compel us to act.

Of course, this deep gut exception is an equal opportunity phenomenon. Perhaps someone should make a poster with Meryl Streep or Halle Berry saying, "A woman's gotta do what a woman's gotta do."

In summary, whether relating to our personal or business lives, if we take the time to evaluate our pursuits on the basis of importance, urgency, and passion, we'll make much better decisions. The ultimate "sweet spot" is when we operate in the high-importance, high-urgency, high-passion quadrant. In that space, doing is easy and fun. In the other spaces, we sometimes have to dig deep to say "no," dig deep to say "yes," or dig deep to get the job done.

Takeaway:

What to do is informed by doing the analysis of what is important, urgent, and moves us to do.

CHAPTER THREE
Do for Yourself

*"Your work is to discover your world and then
with all your heart give yourself to it."*

– Buddha

For most of us, the idea of doing for *others* is fine,
but the idea of doing for *ourselves* sounds… well… self-
indulgent. The truth, however, is that when we're
healthy, happy, and satisfied, we can do more for
ourselves *and* for others. In this chapter, we'll examine
the importance of doing for ourselves, which means
you'll need to suspend your guilt (at least temporarily).

We can't control everything that happens to us in life;

many things are well beyond our control. But that's not to say that we can't significantly affect our course and future. We can. Stephen Covey, a recognized authority on personal effectiveness, wrote, "We are the creative force of our life, and through our own decisions rather than our conditions, if we carefully learn to do certain things, we can accomplish those goals."

Like Covey, I believe we have the power to proactively create our own futures. But that means we must be willing to take the necessary actions—do the things required—to create that future. The best way to see our future is to create it. It's all a matter of choice.

We each choose a profession. We each then choose to excel (or not excel) at that profession. Likewise, barring some uncontrollable illness, we can choose to be healthy. We decide the kind of parent, son, daughter, or spouse we will be just as we decide the kind of citizen we will become. All of these self-states or roles in life begin with a choice, and they're followed by lots of *doing* to turn these choices into realities.

Some years back, a dear friend and a consultant to our bank sent me an intriguing article. His name was Jack, and the article explored and explained the concept of becoming—a notion born in ancient Greece by the philosopher Heraclitus. The gist of the piece was that the joys and fun in life come from doing the things that evolve us into who and what we want to become. Said differently, it's not the achievement of goals that makes life rich and fulfilling, but the journey in pursuit of those goals—it's the *doing* part that counts.

As a business consultant, Jack stressed the importance of long- term strategic planning. This requires deep reflection on the part of company leaders. But, once complete, a good plan articulates a vision for the future and memorializes a company's values that, in turn, are reflected in long, and short-term goals. Finally, most plans of this nature include detailed action items—stepping stones, if you will—necessary to turn the bigger vision into reality.

Without a strategic plan, companies wander. With only a general idea of where they're going, they waste time and resources on non-essential pursuits. But that's not the worst of it. The real price is paid in the opportunities lost. This happens to us as individuals as well, and it's exactly why we should have a *personal* strategic plan of our own.

As a graduate student, one of my favorite professors was Jerry Bell, PhD. He was an accomplished scholar in the field of organizational behavior and a high-value consultant to companies around the globe. He certainly understood the power of strategic planning in business, but also understood the relevance of vision and planning in our personal lives.

One of Dr. Bell's first assignments was to craft a personal strategic plan. He called it a life plan. As part of the assignment, we were instructed to contemplate and articulate key goals we wished to achieve in our lives. Then, we were asked to list the action items we'd need to perform to achieve those goals. He instructed us to be very specific with both goals and action items, which were then plotted on a timeline. Once completed, Dr. Bell encouraged us to periodically update our plans so as to track our progress and to reflect our evolving passions and goals.

No matter how many (or how few) days you have ahead of you, it's never too late to have a life plan. While you can write yours as you see fit, here are a few suggestions as to what you might want to include:

- Purpose statement. What is your stated purpose in life? To arrive at your purpose statement, you might ask yourself questions about what you really want to do with your life or what excites you each day to get up and *do*. An example might be, "To make a true difference with the rest of my life in all the roles in my life."

- Vision for the future. What is your vision for yourself? Who is the person you want to become? An example might be, "To be a healthy and authentic friend to all the people in my life."

- Key goals and objectives. List five or six major goals that are important to you. You might think of them by category. What are your health goals? Family goals? Business goals? Community goals? Do you have any bucket list items?

- Action items for each goal. List three to four tactical action items for each of your listed goals. These are things that must be accomplished to achieve the goal.

Writing a personal statement and vision for the future may seem touchy-feely or even corny. Consequently, this exercise may be a little uncomfortable. But try your best and muscle through it. In my business life, I've experienced the galvanizing power of a well-articulated purpose, vision, set of values, and strategic priorities. In the process, I've discovered that this soft stuff actually matters more than the hard stuff.

After the plan is written, try not to let it sit on the shelf gathering dust (as I did with the life plan I wrote for Dr. Bell). Review it frequently, and update it as changing circumstances and passions dictate. Most importantly, do the things that make the plan come true, and create the future you want. As they say in business, "plan your work, then work your plan." The power is *doing* it.

Takeaway:

We can create the life we desire if we plan and then do.

CHAPTER FOUR
Do Be Healthy

*"A healthy body creates a healthy mind. A
healthy mind creates a healthy body"*

— The Author

We've all heard that healthy bodies create healthy minds. It's a fact. Now, there's a new field of medicine that suggests the reciprocal is also true—that a healthy mind creates a healthy body. In fact, scientific support for the mind-body connection is overwhelming. Scholarly books and articles confirm that doing the right things to care for our bodies has healthy benefits for our minds. This means that good health necessarily contemplates both body and mind. But to create this virtuous cycle, we must engage our *do*.

HEALTHY BODY

Achieving and maintaining good health isn't always easy, but it can be much easier—and even enjoyable—if we decide it matters. It takes time, persistence, and discipline. The everyday demands of life have a way of getting in the way and foiling our best intentions to do the things necessary to remain fit.

Time constraints, motivational challenges, and common vices are but a few of the impediments. Besides that, diet and exercise don't exactly swing the pleasure meter the way that other (less healthy) pursuits can. Fortunately, some new inexpensive technologies can help. The ones I find most useful are those that help me monitor the calories I take in and the calories I burn. In essence, they improve my self-awareness, which in turn empowers me to exert greater control.

When it comes to exercise, I use two devices. The first is called a Fitbit. Worn on a belt or wrist, it monitors the steps taken during the course of the day and calculates the calories burned as a result.

In my experience, wearing the Fitbit creates an inexplicable motivation to sit less, ride less, walk more, and burn more calories. Now, I walk places I would previously have driven whether it's to the grocery, drug store, or lunch spot. This creates a nice workout while completing a necessary task at the same time. (Though reluctant to admit it, I even compete with myself to better the previous day's record.

Most doctors say that walking is the best physical activity we can do for ourselves. For what it's worth, Thomas Jefferson shared the same opinion. "Walking is the best possible exercise," he said. Charles Dickens did as well and, in fact, was said to have walked over 20 miles per day.

The second bit of technology I employ to help monitor and manage my exercise and diet is a smartphone calorie counter. I simply enter what I eat into my phone app. At the end of the day, I push a button to learn the number of calories I've consumed. Matched against the calorie burn count from the Fitbit, I get a pretty good picture of my net calories for the day. Employing this simple process, I've found that weight loss and weight gain are no longer mysteries.

Of course, none of this can happen unless and until we actually do it. We must enter the data, do the math, adjust our activities, and diet accordingly. Most of all, we must stay disciplined.

Besides motivation, our second biggest impediment to exercise is finding the time to do it. It's a constant and ongoing challenge for all of us. My solution is to schedule exercise the same way I do lunch dates, doctors' appointments, conference calls, or business meetings. Over the past 20 years, I've marked my calendar almost every day with a three-letter acronym known only to a few close co-workers and me—DTS. It means "down the street" for exercise.

My DTS time can be a mid-morning work out, a lunchtime run, or a late afternoon walk. I do it wherever I am. Whether at home or on the road, I always have a pair of running/walking shoes within reach. I walk every day and I love it. (Yes, I'm the guy people see walking in the rain when it's 20 degrees outside.)

President Kennedy once said, "Physical fitness is not only one of the most important keys to a healthy body, it is the basis of dynamic and creative intellectual activity." The last three words, "creative intellectual activity," describe a healthy mind in its most powerful state. Creativity combined with a big dose of *do* leads to breakthrough ideas and innovative solutions to our biggest challenges in life. Moreover, it provokes us to ask questions we didn't know existed.

As discussed, a healthy mind contributes to a healthy body just as a healthy body facilitates a healthy mind. It's a mutually beneficial cycle of body helping mind and mind helping body.

The notion that a healthy mind fosters a healthy body is not a new concept. 4000 years ago physicians in China noticed that illnesses frequently followed periods of frustration in the lives of their patients. Today there are growing fields of medicine with big names like neuroimmunology and behavioral cardiology that are based on the notion that our bodies reflect our emotions and "feel" the stress we carry.

In their most extreme forms, the effects of stress can cause heart attacks, illnesses of all types, weight gain, severe stomach problems, and crippling depression. All of this prevents us from doing the things that make us healthy and happy. They impede us from achieving the ultimate objective: a healthy mind in a healthy body.

Dr. Arthur Barsky, professor of psychiatry at Harvard Medical School, has written a book called *Worried Sick: Our Troubled Quest for Wellness*. In it, he writes, "We 'burn' with anger, 'tremble' with fear, feel 'choked up' with sadness; our 'stomachs turn' with revulsion. Everyone tends to experience unpleasant emotions as unpleasant bodily symptoms and thus to feel physically distressed when emotionally distressed."

As Dr. Barsky explains, there's a growing acceptance of the mind-body connection within the medical field; an increasing number of psychological treatment options at most hospitals; and an understanding that treating the mind is just as important as treating the body.

So, what can one do to create a healthy mind in a healthy body? Answer: Plenty. We can start by exploring and understanding well- established techniques such as self-soothing, stress management, and relaxation training as well as cognitive therapy practices like meditation and guided imagery.

Exercise is considered one of the best therapies for stress. However, I've discovered an equally powerful tool called mindfulness. In my experience, it requires more discipline than physical exercise. Though often taught independent of religion, mindfulness is a form of Buddhist meditation. I first learned of it at the Canyon Ranch in Tucson, Arizona—a sort of health and wellness camp for adults.

I describe mindfulness as an exercise because it is. Since the 1970s, clinical psychologists and psychiatrists have used it to treat those suffering from a variety of psychological conditions. It's been most effective, however, in reducing anxiety and stress and in the treatment of depression. While in the Sonora Desert, I also learned of (and began practicing) biofeedback. Basically, it's the process of controlling thoughts and emotions to manipulate certain physiological functions like heart rate, brainwaves, muscle tone, skin conductance, and pain perception. Among other things, it's been effective in treating headaches and migraines.

By nature, I am tightly wound. Even so, it's my choice as to whether I remain this way. That's why I decided to do something about it and began to incorporate these various stress-relieving techniques and even employed the professional assistance of a biofeedback expert.

My biofeedback expert recommended that I purchase a few inexpensive tools to help me monitor my heart rate during deep breathing and relaxation sessions. In effect, these tools measure my ability to control stress and anxiety (or as my son puts it, my ability to chill).

The exercises I've learned help me to be quiet, still, and achieve a level of calmness that I don't experience during a normal workday. Make no mistake, this process hasn't been easy given my shortcomings. But I know the benefits, and I'm committed to making improvements.

Healthcare professionals tell me—and I have experienced it— that one can gain the same benefits of meditation while walking. The trick is to focus on breathing rather than the normal thoughts that create stress. There are also many good apps and guided meditation recordings that can be purchased or even downloaded for free. With a smartphone and a set of ear buds, you're set to experiment with what works for you.

Talk of meditation can make some folks uneasy. But it shouldn't. The Bible has a similar message to those who find it difficult to relax. It's found in Psalm 46:10, and it reads, "Be still and know that I am GOD."

Attitude is another big contributor to health. Research in this sub-specialty of mind-body medicine confirms that attitude has everything to do with a healthy body. From time-to-time we all hear stories of people with serious illness who face their challenges with positive, inspiring courage. But attitude can do more than help fight existing illness; it can help prevent illnesses before they develop.

Positive attitudes are grounded in the belief that tomorrow will be better. This, in turn, thwarts the corrosive effects of anger, resentment, and stress, thereby promoting a healthier body and happier life.

The good news for anyone who struggles with attitude is that attitude—like *do*—is a choice.

Takeaway:

**The mind and body are mutually dependent.
Exercise and maintain them both.**

CHAPTER FIVE

Do in Business

"A business that makes nothing but money is a poor business."

— Henry Ford

With the passage of the 13th Amendment, we each have the right to decide for ourselves *what* we do for a living and *for whom* we do it. Consequently, when we exercise personal discretion and elect to work for an organization or business, we have the obligation to do what we can to promote, improve, and advance that enterprise.

When we take a vested interest in improving the companies for whom we work, we acquire a sense of ownership. We feel vested and part of the organization. In doing so, we're rewarded with a deeper sense of satisfaction. This makes us better employees and even elevates the game of those around us. Besides that, it enhances our value to the company and improves our own chances for advancement.

Early in my career, I recall hearing friends and colleagues describe the business issues and challenges faced by their respective employers. Sometimes these were followed by good— even brilliant—ideas as to how problems could be resolved or addressed. Though occasionally someone would tell of elevating a suggestion to management, more often than not they took no such initiative. In my observation, their passivity was driven by fear: fear of looking stupid, fear of offending management, fear of appearing too eager, etc. These were irrational fears, of course, and none were viable excuses for not attempting to promote, improve, or advance their respective companies.

Disinterested managers certainly exist. However, there's always someone in the chain of command who's motivated and receptive to thoughtful ideas, particularly when proffered in a constructive manner by a well-meaning employee. I call this leading from the middle, and anyone can do it. These are the employees— the team members— who are the real leaders regardless of what title they hold.

The principles of do are as relevant, applicable, and empowering to us as employees, managers, and executives as they are in our personal lives. But nothing happens, of course, unless we take action and do!

DO BE AN ENTREPRENEUR

Not everyone is disposed to working for someone else. Some folk have the risk tolerance and disposition to strike out on their own. If this is your calling—to be an entrepreneur—there's one quality you can't do without: you'll need to be a doer.

Steve Jobs, the founder of Apple, was the quintessential entrepreneur. Having truly started his company in a (proverbial) garage before building it into one of the world's largest and most admired companies, Mr. Jobs embodied Apple's "Think Different" message: "The people who think they are crazy enough to change the world are the ones who do."

About ten years ago, a team of former co-workers and I decided to start a private fund to invest in small businesses. Our purpose was to provide growth capital to businesses that were too small to access the public markets (i.e., the stock and bond markets). When we began our pursuit, we had several big unknowns. First, we didn't know if we could raise the money required to create our fund. Second, we didn't know if we could secure the necessary license to operate as a small business investment company from the Small Business Administration (SBA). The SBA's process was tedious and highly selective, particularly for first-time applicants.

Despite the unknowns, we passionately charged ahead. We submitted our application and began calling on investors with all of the professional persistence and positive audacity we could muster. We believed whole-heartedly that we could give our investors an attractive return on their investments while helping small businesses grow and create jobs. We worked feverishly for an entire year without taking a single dollar in compensation and, in fact, funded the business with our own savings.

Over a decade has passed since we launched our business. Today, we manage more than $500 million on behalf of a great cast of investors and we recently launched our third investment fund. In 2013, we were even named the Small Business Investment Company of the Year by the SBA—a national award.

I'm certainly proud of our accomplishments, but my purpose is not to boast. Instead, I tell our story to emphasize the critical importance of do when starting a new business. Successful businesses are launched and built when an individual entrepreneur (or team of entrepreneurs in our case) decides to do in spite of the risks and uncertainties.

Every business venture starts with a business idea. But great ideas go nowhere unless and until someone does something to make it happen.

DO FOR THE GREATER GOOD

Successful businesses provide products and services that we value—or at least someone values. (Otherwise, they wouldn't be successful.) In and of itself, that's good. As a businessman operating in the often-vilified private capital world, I submit that venture capital, private equity, and private debt are good things—they provide the necessary capital for business formation and growth. Furthermore, the kind of good discussed in this section goes far beyond providing a product or service that's in demand; businesses can be (and should be) instruments of good for their communities as well.

Early in my career as a banker, I came to see and experience the good that we could do beyond the services we provided to clients. At the time, my company sponsored a Teacher of the Year Award. It was given to the best public school teacher in each of the cities in which we operated. It was a terrific initiative that recognized those unsung professionals who play such a critical role in the development of our children and, ultimately, in shaping our society.

We also supported an initiative called The Program of Excellence in Education. It was a non-profit organization that, among other things, raised funds for public school teachers to help them purchase necessary supplies. (Teachers often purchase supplies using their personal dollars.) One project was as simple as providing art supplies such as crayons and paper to kids who couldn't afford the basics.

Contributing businesses, like ours, were encouraged to present their checks in person so they could see and appreciate how their contributions were making a difference. I made the delivery for our company and can still see the radiant smiles from teachers and students alike. It was a wonderful feeling to belong to an organization that made a difference. The coup de grace, however, came when we received our thank you notes. They were written on the same art paper and using the same crayons purchased with our funding. This is what I call a "little big thing" (two words strung together that are not oxymoronic).

Over the years, I've employed the collective power of my co-workers and company's financial resources to do good things for programs ranging from Boy Scouts to homeless shelters to YMCAs.

Good companies feel the responsibility to do more than take care of their customers and their own. They harness their power to do good for their communities as well.

Takeaway:

Businesses can be instruments of good, and each of us has the ability to influence and leverage this potential.

CHAPTER SIX

Do for Your Community

"Ask not what your country can do for you. Ask what you can do for your country."

— John F. Kennedy

In previous chapters, I've touched on the concept of doing for our respective communities. In this context, "community" is meant to confer more than just one's own neighborhood. It's a flexible, broader, and more comprehensive term that can mean a town, city, or state. Sometimes the effect of our actions can even be national or (in exceptional cases) global.

In 1994, I listened as a young woman described a bold and ambitious vision for an organization called Teach for

America. At the time, I'd never heard of it. Now, however, given the organization's success in the intervening years, Teach for America is a household name. Moreover, its founder, Wendy Kopp, epitomizes the notion of giving back and doing for one's community.

As a 21-year-old college senior, Ms. Kopp observed the poor quality of public education in low-income areas and set her sights on changing it. Her idea was to create an avenue— similar in respects to the Peace Corps—that recruited top-notch college students with an opportunity to make a difference ... immediately. They would serve their communities as front-line teachers in these challenged schools.

Of course, good ideas are a dime-a-dozen. Unless they're followed by action, they go nowhere. Looking back, Wendy Kopp describes her biggest asset as her youth and inexperience. (I say she hadn't yet learned what couldn't be done!) Engaging her do, she organized a conference at which she described the problem and her vision for a solution. People liked what they heard, and within a year she raised enough funds from individuals, foundations, and corporations to commence operations and recruit 500 college graduates.

Today, over 33,000 talented, energetic, and motivated teachers are making a difference in schools across the country thanks to the vision and efforts of Wendy Kopp and Teach for America. As American cultural anthropologist Margaret Mead once said, "Never doubt that a small group of thoughtful, committed citizens can change the world: Indeed, it's the only thing that ever has."

A hero of mine is James B. Hunt, former governor of North Carolina. He grew up on a farm in rural North Carolina before attending North Carolina State College (now North Carolina State University) where he was elected student body president. After finishing school, he practiced law. Soon thereafter, however, Jim Hunt felt the call to public service and became the youngest lieutenant governor in North Carolina history. Subsequently, he served two terms as governor after which he returned to practicing law. Notwithstanding the economic incentives to remain in private practice, Jim Hunt returned to public service and served two more terms as governor.

It wasn't the power (and it certainly wasn't the money)

that compelled Jim Hunt to spend sixteen years as the CEO of North Carolina. Instead, he was motivated by a sense of purpose and service to do all he could do for his community. His accomplishments were many but, arguably, his most important were in the field of education.

Even after leaving public office, Jim Hunt continues to serve. At 77, he remains THE Governor and still works tirelessly on issues of statewide and national concern. He founded the Institute for Emerging Issues (IEI), which hosts an annual forum, attracting thought leaders from around the world. Reflecting Governor Hunt's commitment to think and actually do something in response, he appropriately refers to IEI as a "think and do tank."

I went to see Governor Hunt while researching this book. I asked him what keeps him working 10 hours a day on issues and endeavors affecting his community, home state, and the nation. He replied without the slightest hesitation. "Because there is so much left to do."

During one of Jim Hunt's IEI forums, former President Clinton told a humorous but insightful story about his friend, Governor Hunt. In the aftermath of Hurricane

Floyd—a devastating storm that caused massive flooding in Eastern North Carolina—then Governor Hunt made daily calls to the White House until disaster money reached his beleaguered state. Jim Hunt was clearly a doer who did what was necessary under the circumstances.

My family was among those affected by Hurricane Floyd. We had five feet of water in our house, and like thousands of others, we were forced to move out and rebuild. But what I learned from the experience is that disaster has a way of bringing out the best in people. Wonderful people came from all over the country to help flood victims like me.

During the post-Floyd recovery there was no black or white, rich or poor. Neither was there any judgment attached to where one lived. There was only a sense of do. What can I do to help my neighbors rebuild their lives? I witnessed first-hand the good in others and the compelling desire to do something to help. We all have this capacity, and there's no reason to wait for a flood to show it.

One doesn't need to be a national figure to accomplish big things. In a recent Washington Post article, Sportswriter John Feinstein related a story that took place in the mid-1960s involving an assistant basketball coach at the University of North Carolina.

Even though UNC (the oldest public university in the country by the way) had been admitting African-American students for over a decade, Chapel Hill was still a segregated town. While African-American students were (somewhat) accepted on campus, it was a different story off campus. The restaurants along Franklin Street catered to white customers only.

Unsatisfied with what he witnessed and undeterred by the political and social norms of the day, this young assistant basketball coach decided to do what he could do to bring about effectuate change. After discussing the matter with his pastor, Reverend Robert Seymour, he decided to act—to do!

Accompanied by Reverend Seymour and a black member of the church, the young coach entered a Chapel Hill restaurant and asked to be served. To the amazement of many, they were indeed served. It was the beginning of the end for segregation in Chapel Hill.

A few years later, that assistant coach became the head

coach at the University of North Carolina and, today, the UNC basketball arena bears his name: The Dean Smith Center.

After reading Mr. Feinstein's article, I visited Dr. Robert Seymour to discuss this experience. Though fifty years have passed since that evening with (then) Assistant Coach Dean Smith, his recollection was crisp and clear.

During our discussion, Dr. Seymour spoke of the contrast at the time between the enlightened university and the (as yet) unenlightened community around it. He then recited a quote from Frank Porter Graham—a former U.S. senator and former president of the University of North Carolina. "Chapel Hill is like a lighthouse casting its beam into the darkness. But like a lighthouse, it too is dark at its bottom."

Coach Smith and Dr. Seymour did what they could to change the system—to shine light into the bottom of the lighthouse so-to-speak, and they succeeded. Within five years of their bold courageous action, Chapel Hill elected its first black mayor.

According to Feinstein, when Coach Smith was later

commended for this action, Smith offered a surprising response. "You should never be proud of doing what's right," he said. "You should just do what's right."

I certainly can't compare myself to Presidential Medal of Freedom recipient Dean Smith (or anyone else I reference or cite in this book). I have, however, done my best to give back to my community and can attest to the deep satisfaction derived from doing it. It was something I began in my hometown of Rocky Mount, North Carolina. Once I started, there was no reason to stop.

I was a young banker in my twenties when I moved back to Rocky Mount. It was where I had grown up and where I had acquired a sense of obligation to my community by watching my father. He was a wonderful mentor, and he taught me the importance of giving back, caring for others, and good human relations.

Following my father's example, I became an active contributor to numerous community causes and organizations. I volunteered my time and services to the United Way, my church, the YMCA, the Boy Scouts, the Chamber of Commerce, and many other non-profits that did good things in the area.

In the years since, I've served my university in various capacities, and my home state as an economic advisor to a governor and on various statewide boards. One of those boards is the North Carolina Community Foundation, a non-profit that encourages and supports families and organizations that want to establish foundations or planned gifts for the benefit of their communities.

Most community foundations work the same way: donors choose the specific causes and charities they wish to support, while the community foundation manages the distributions to ensure that the donor's wishes are carried out. In my experience, they are excellent mechanisms for giving back.

I've learned much from my involvement with these organizations. In the beginning, however, when approached to serve in a new capacity, I sometimes felt unprepared—even inadequate—to do the job. But once in the game, I learned quickly and gained confidence. Eventually, my fears dissipated. Now, I'm not afraid to serve on any board at any level. In fact, I love the challenge and relish the opportunity to learn and grow.

The point of this personal story is to demonstrate that, regardless of experience or background, we all have the capacity to give back to our communities. All it takes is a little motivation and a willingness to serve—to do.

Every time I've taken on a community project I've been enriched. But the rewards for community service are different from those received from business or personal accomplishments. All feel great, but community achievements confer a deeper level of satisfaction. Winston Churchill may have captured it best when he said, "We make a living by what we get, but we make a life by what we give."

Before reading John Feinstein's remarkable story of Dean Smith, I was quite proud of my civic and community involvements. Now, however, I view these contributions in a different light. I do my best to check my pride at the door (and leave it to my wonderful and loving mother to be proud of my actions).

Takeaway:

Our deepest level of satisfaction and highest sense of accomplishment come from doing for our communities.

CHAPTER SEVEN

Don't Overdo It

"Moderation in all things, especially moderation."
— Ralph Waldo Emerson

This book is about doing, action, and getting it done. Yet, living a life of *do* doesn't mean we should run full-tilt all the time. Moderation and good sense are as applicable to *do* as they are to any other pursuit, activity, or belief. A life of *do* should emphasize balance and moderation.

Doing (or attempting) too much has real risks and consequences, including decreased effectiveness and diminishing marginal returns as well as adverse mental and physical effects. I know from experience because moderation has never come easy for me.

DECREASED EFFECTIVENESS

When we cram too many ambitions into a given period, something has to give. Often, it's quality and effectiveness. Hence, a system (like the Do Wedge©) for filtering out many items and prioritizing others becomes critically important.

In business, too many initiatives can lead to poor execution. This, in turn, increases the risk of falling short of larger goals and the realization of company objectives. Business scholars and consultants often suggest that a person or business should set only three to five major objectives each year … not ten, twenty, or thirty. Each key objective is built upon three to five key action items that must be accomplished for the objective to be reached.

Doing the math, five major objectives each supported by five key tactical action items produce a to-do list of 25-high priority items. That's plenty. Any more and the likely result is diminished effectiveness.

DIMINISHING MARGINAL RETURNS

Biting off more than we can reasonably chew can also result in diminishing marginal returns. Basically, the law of diminishing marginal returns, as it's known in economic circles, holds that if we keep adding more of one factor of production while holding all others constant, eventually we'll experience lower per-unit returns.

Twisted slightly to make the point, adding more and more to-do items to our list will eventually result in fewer items being accomplished per unit of time spent. That is, unless we're willing to compromise on the quality. Figure 2 expresses the notion in visual terms.

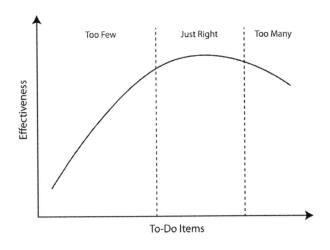

The vertical axis reflects the overall effectiveness of our efforts. The horizontal axis depicts the number of to-dos. Understanding our personal limits and finding our sweet spot may involve a little trial-and-error but, over time, we find it.

The trick, of course, is to operate at the precipice of the curve. That requires us to dial back our commitments by actively and thoughtfully culling items before they ever make our to-do lists. This frees us up to allocate time to things that really matter and increases our operating effectiveness.

Businesses can over-do it too. "The essence of strategy is choosing what not to do," said Harvard Business School professor Michael Porter. When companies have too many competing priorities they lose focus. This diminishes the company's effectiveness with respect to important strategic objectives.

HEALTH IMPACT

Not only do we compromise effectiveness when we attempt to do too much, but we place our mental and physical health in jeopardy as well.

When the human heart receives disorganized electrical impulses, cardiologists call it fibrillation. In essence, the heart beats irregularly and too fast. Even though a fibrillating heart works much harder than a normal heart, it's less efficient in actually pumping blood.

We too can reach a point at which we're fibrillating—working harder and harder but accomplishing less. When this happens, we feel harried, overwhelmed, ineffective, and, more than anything, stressed. Stress and anxiety have many effects on our mental and physical well-being—none of which are good.

Stress can lead to explosive behavior and depression not to mention unhealthy coping mechanisms such as over-eating, smoking, drug usage, and alcohol abuse. As previously discussed, stress goes from our brains to our bodies and can cause exhaustion, headaches, stomach problems, and a host of other ailments. The good news is that we can actually control the stress we put upon ourselves.

Overdoing is self-imposed. It's a choice, and the first

step toward controlling and limiting stress is awareness. Beyond that, here are a few things we can do to help keep it in check:

- Perform an honest daily, weekly, or monthly review of your to-do list. Ask yourself: Is it too ambitious? Is it too long? If so, make adjustments.

- At work, limit your list of personal and business objectives to an important few. Three to five is a good target.

- Take the time each day to feel what your body is telling you. If you're overdoing it, your body will let you know. But you can only hear what your body is saying if you're actually listening.

- Apply the same discipline of moderation to your do activities as you would (should) in every other aspect of life.

Life is really a long list of to-do items. Guard and manage your list carefully. Be thoughtful and disciplined when deciding what goes on it, and always take care not to overdo it.

Takeaway:

Overdoing can lead to diminished effectiveness and negative health consequences. *Don't* do it.

CHAPTER EIGHT

Heeding the Call to Do

"Inaction breeds doubt and fear. Action breeds confidence and courage. If you want to conquer fear, do not sit home and think about it. Go out and get busy."

— Dale Carnegie

It takes no courage to be a spectator and watch as life passes by. Likewise, it takes no courage to acknowledge a duty but ignore it; witness a wrong but do nothing; or observe a community need then wait for others to address it.

Doing involves risk. Sometimes the risk is unavoidable, and sometimes the risks are considerable. Consequently, doing takes courage.

DUTY AND IMPACT

Whether or not we acknowledge it, we all have duties—as parents, as spouses, as partners, as community members, and as citizens—and these duties can be effective motivators for *do*. George Washington once said, "Happiness and moral duty are inseparably connected." This form of happiness is achieved by *acting* upon an observed duty. This, in turn, leads to healthy pride and self-respect—both important componentsof happiness.

Service to country in time of war is the ultimate *do*. The brave men and women who volunteered for military service during World War II understood the meaning. My father was among them. Given that he was only 17 when he volunteered, I once asked him where he had found the courage. "It was the right thing to do," he replied without expression. "I felt I had to do it." We should never overlook, minimize, or fail to appreciate the courage and service of those who act upon this duty.

Former Soviet leader and Nobel laureate Mikhail Gorbachev had courage. When he pushed to reform the Soviet system during the 1980s, he met considerable opposition from hardliners. His policies of *glasnost* (increased openness) and *perestroika* (restructuring) ultimately led to the demise of the Warsaw Pact and dissolution of the Soviet Union. Notwithstanding subsequent developments in Russia, Mr. Gorbachev was a courageous man. "If not me, who? And if not now, when?" he once said.

"CHANGING THE WORLD" IMPACT

Microsoft founder Bill Gates is one of the wealthiest men in the world. In addition to his business successes, his greatest legacy may well be the humanitarian accomplishments of the charitable foundation that he and his wife, Melinda, established in 1997. One of the most ambitious projects funded by The Bill and Melinda Gates Foundation has been the Global Polio Eradication Initiative.

With the stated purpose of eradicating polio *worldwide*, the challenge seemed almost too big to overcome. Yet, with the help of Bill and Melinda Gates, tremendous progress has been made. Over 2.5 billion children have been immunized, and the incidence of this cruel disease (that once paralyzed 1000 children per day across 125 countries) has been reduced by 99%.

Bono, the lead singer for U2, has used his celebrity to improve the lives of countless Africans. He forged partnerships with Congress and multiple presidents to deal with the poverty and debt in numerous African nations. "As a rock star, I have two instincts," he once said. "I want to have fun, and I want to change the world. I have a chance to do both,"

But one doesn't need to be a world leader or rock star to change the world. Consider the case of a 42-year-old seamstress who refused to give up her seat for white passengers on a segregated bus in 1955. In the case of Rosa Parks, one person's actions started a chain reaction that ultimately changed the country and the world. "I have learned over the years that when one's mind is made up, this diminishes fear," she later said of her decision not to give up her seat. "Knowing what must be done does away with fear."

Though millions of Americans recognized that segregation

was wrong, Rosa Parks had the courage to do something about it. Her courageous actions are said to have marked the beginning of the Civil Rights Movement.

A WORD ON NOT DOING

Inaction—doing nothing—is a choice. When we choose not to act (when we really should), the consequences can be every bit as harmful and destructive as actively pursuing the wrong path.

Sometimes, but not often, the consequences of our inaction are monstrous. Consider the years preceding the Holocaust when the Nazi regime incrementally and systematically dehumanized then destroyed the Jews of Europe. Along the way, many otherwise good people watched but did nothing.

Closer to home, consider the years preceding and during our own Civil Rights Movement. As Martin Luther King, Jr., put it, "History will have to record that the greatest tragedy of this period of social transition was not the strident clamor of the bad people, but the appalling silence of the good people."

Of course, not all inaction results in death and destruction. More commonly, the results are unnecessary pain, loss, or hardship for others. It happens all of the time. Here are a few examples:

- When we see something that we know is wrong, yet we are silent and do nothing.

- When we observe a problem in our community or workplace, then wait on others to do something about it.

- When we pass on an opportunity to serve our community in some capacity.

- When we fail to help others in distress when we have the ability and means to do it.

- When we're aware of an existing wrong, but remain silent.

We don't have to be an elected official or even the person in charge to tackle the wrongs or address the needs we witness. Just speak up and do what you can.

Recognizing situations that call for action isn't always easy. Sometimes the need is obvious; it screams for our attention. Other times the need is less overt; it speaks in a faint whisper.

Theodore Roosevelt once said, "In any moment of decision, the best thing you can do is the right thing. The worst thing you can do is nothing." Similarly, the Bible says, "So whoever knows the right thing to do and fails to do it, for him it is a sin." (James 4:17).

More often than not, we pay the price for our own inaction. The price paid is usually opportunities lost. Examples include:

- Not exercising because the bed feels too good to get up and going.

- Not making progress on a big personal goal.

- Not reaching out to our mother, father, daughter, or son because we just don't make the time.

- Not moving on a project that could enhance our in the workplace.

- Not seeking professional medical advice when there's good reason to think we should.

I once heard a speech given in honor of a man who had lived a good long life serving his community. In closing, the speaker referred to (what I describe as) a nursing home reflection. He said that although no one looks forward to living in a nursing home, we might nevertheless live long enough to some day find ourselves at an advanced age, lying in a bed, and quietly reflecting on life. "When that time comes, how will you reflect back on the things you did or didn't do?" he asked. "Will you have regrets or will you smile when you recall how you lived life for yourself and others?"

It's my belief that when that nursing home moment arrives, most of us will measure the things we did do against the things we didn't do. Our conclusions will reflect the net difference between the two.

Takeaway:

Action requires courage, something we all have within us. Find it. Then do what you can to change the world.

CHAPTER NINE

Do's Biggest Foes

"Never put off until tomorrow what you can do the day after tomorrow."

— Mark Twain

Procrastination is one impediment—but not the only impediment—to a life of *do*. Others include fear, over thinking, and lack of time.

FEAR

Fear is the greatest impediment to doing, and it appears in a variety of forms. There's the fear that we can't achieve the contemplated pursuit, the fear that we're somehow inadequate and not up to the task, and the fear and discomfort that comes from taking on an unfamiliar task. Finally, there's the fear of how others will react to our efforts.

It's said that as many as three of every four people fear public speaking. It even has a name, glossophobia, and it exemplifies how fear can grip us and impede our ability to *do*.

I understand this particular fear very well. At times in my career, I've experienced all the symptoms—sweating, shortness of breath, and general anxiety—in anticipation of a talk or speech. The only way I overcame that fear was to do it and keep doing it. With each delivery, I grew stronger and more confident. With each delivery, I breached another hole in my wall of fear. Today, my fear is under control but a healthy level strike still lingers. It's just enough to make me prepare and practice.

Practicing an action that creates fear is the best way to cure it. Like exercise, practice is doing, and with each attempt, we make incremental progress. Even the best athletes in the world—irrespective of the sport—continue to practice. They also seek advice and assistance from coaches. Even after winning 18 major golf championships,

Jack Nicklaus continued to take golf lessons! Practice, coaching, and doing diminish fear and improve our effectiveness.

An emotion akin to fear is discomfort. Twenty years ago, I read Jim Collins' best-selling book entitled *Built to Last*. One chapter (and one sentence in particular) stuck with me after all these years. In describing companies that last for decades, Collins writes:

[The best and most visionary companies] install powerful mechanisms to increase discomfort and stimulate change before the external environment demands it. They worry about becoming fat, lazy and complacent.

In the same book, Collins introduced the concept of big hairy audacious goals—"BHAG" for short. Goals like this can scare us. They conjure fears that "we're no match" for the task at hand. The really big ones induce equally big fears of failure.

Whether in business or in our personal lives, the challenge we all face is to understand our fears then take them on. We must move beyond our comfort zones and embrace the discomfort. If we try but fail, we learn and then try again.

Fear is a deep and hard-to-describe feeling, but it's most often grounded in irrational thought and unsubstantiated assumptions. When a seemingly impermeable wall of fear appears, taking a moment to examine and understand the fear we're experiencing is the first step in overcoming it. In these situations, we should ask ourselves:

- What are the consequences of failure?

- Why am I afraid?

- Is the *do* action/goal really that hard?

- How good will I feel if I don't get it done?

Fear is natural, and a little fear is healthy. It prompts us to take stock of the risks we're facing. It should also prompt us to discern real risks from perceived risks so that we can prepare for the former and dismiss the latter.

PROCRASTINATION

Another impediment to doing is procrastination. The fact is that some things just aren't fun to do, but they're nevertheless important (i.e., high importance but low passion quadrant in our Do Wedge©). This is where we experience the strongest propensity to procrastinate.

Procrastination is a subject that's been studied

extensively and about which much is written. Some psychologists suggest that procrastination is a subconscious mechanism that prevents us from doing harm to ourselves—it keeps us safe or in some cases even helps us make better decisions. While I'm sure that procrastination has saved a few people from making bad decisions, I'm convinced that the downside of being a procrastinator far outweighs the upside.

So, what can we do to overcome—or at least minimize—our tendency to procrastinate so that it doesn't impede us from fulfilling our goals and ambitions? The best answer I've found is in a book entitled *Procrastination: Why You Do It, What To Do About It* by Jane Burka and Lenora Yuen.

Burka and Yuen offer a simple four-step process for conquering procrastination as follows:

1. Realize you're delaying something unnecessarily.

2. Discover the real reasons for your delay, then list them out.

3. Dispute those real reasons and overcome them.

4. Begin the task.

I particularly like Burka and Yuen's suggestion that we list our reasons for procrastinating. Seeing them on paper makes them easier to address, discount, and eliminate. I also like their recommendation that we argue with ourselves about ways to overcome our procrastination drivers.

I hesitate to suggest this last form of procrastination, but it certainly exists and, therefore, must be addressed. For lack of a better term, I call it laziness. In one of my favorite books by Pat Conroy, *Beach Music*, he writes, "The pursuit of greatness means that laziness has no place in your life." I certainly believe it to be true.

Laziness is a disinclination to *do* despite having an ability to *do*. While we all have the right to be lazy from time-to-time, we shouldn't let it prevent us from doing the things that are important.

In my experience, snapping out of a temporary state of laziness begins with self-awareness. When I feel lazy, I try to get up and get moving physically. My hope is to get the blood flowing enough to muster a better mood or attitude. Sometimes I succeed, and sometimes I don't. But I do try.

ANALYSIS PARALYSIS

A third impediment to doing is analysis paralysis. (We partially addressed this issue in Chapter Two discussing Mr. Lencioni's concept of seeking "clarity over certainty.") When deciding whether to undertake or not undertake a particular pursuit, it's easy to get stuck analyzing the situation. Doing your homework to evaluate and prepare is good and important. However, once you've done enough analysis to become reasonably informed, it's time to make a decision and move forward—one way or another.

Again, that's not to say we shouldn't intelligently analyze and consider our pursuits. We should. The process should resemble a one-man chess game. If you haven't seen one, the player analyzes his (or her) move on one side of the table, then moves to the other side and repeats the process. The important thing is to be objective and strategic while keeping the process moving forward. Some of the questions we might ask when evaluating a pursuit include the following:

- Is the information we have sufficient?

- Is the information credible?

- Have we thought through the downside?

- Do we know the upside, and is it worth the risk?

In business, analysis is frequently thought to be a numbers game—numbers drive the decisions. But in truth, numbers don't make decisions, people do. As Peter Drucker—the thought leader of modern business and creator of Management by Objectives— once put it, "Whenever you see a successful business, someone once made a courageous decision."

The courage to *do* is informed by analysis, but it shouldn't be crippled by analysis. This concept is as crucial and applicable to our personal lives as it is in business. The goals and objectives expressed in a life plan should reflect careful thought and a healthy dose of analysis. But an obsession with analysis will leave us paralyzed.

If our dreams and ambitions are never converted into to- do items, they'll never be achieved. So, let's do the proper and prudent amount of analysis on the things that matter to us, then get on with it—and do it!

TIME

The last impediment to *do* is time.

We all have constraints—legitimate constraints—on our

time. But, "I don't have time" is way over used as an excuse for not getting important things done. The solution is to exercise greater discretion when deciding what's worth doing and what's not.

If something isn't worth pursuing, then promptly discard it, and don't look back. If it is worth pursuing, then prioritize it against other pursuits using a process like the one outlined in chapter two (the Do Wedge©) and deal with it accordingly. Along the way, try to keep these tidbits in mind:

- Put to-do items on your calendar (like I do for exercise).

- If it's really important, make a time slot on your calendar just as you would an important business meeting

- Thoughtfully allocate the amount of time the pursuit will take, then stick to it and do it.

- Be spontaneous and responsive to others, but protect your time as the precious resource it is.

There are certainly instances when lack of time is a valid excuse. Often, however, "I didn't *have* time" really means, "I didn't *make* time." If we actively manage our time with thoughtful self-awareness and discipline, we'll find that time is not a barrier to accomplishing the things that are most important to us.

Takeaway:

Fear and time can be impediments to *do*, but both can be overcome with a little planning and courage.

CHAPTER TEN
The Golden Rule

"Do unto others as you would have them do unto you."
— Luke 6:31

The Golden Rule—the maxim that we should treat others the way we'd like to be treated—isn't exclusive to Christian or even Judeo-Christian traditions. In one form or another, it's an expression that's reflected in all of the world's major religions and, according to British philosopher Simon Blackburn, in almost every ethical convention as well.

In a complicated world where right and wrong can seem like incremental shades of gray, the beauty of the Golden Rule is its simplicity. At least when it comes to how we interact with others, the Golden Rule distills the decision-making process down to one simple question: "How would I like to be treated?" For anyone living a life of do, this is more than a standard of conduct; it's an affirmative call to action. Within reason, we should do for others what we would have them do for us.

The effort expended doing for others doesn't have to be great to have an effect. An unsolicited compliment or kind word is a good example. If sincerely offered with no strings attached, they can lift our spirits, change our perceptions, and even prompt us to do the same for others. Why then wouldn't the Golden Rule impel us to do this for others? Answer: It should!

During a training course, I once took on the subject of business leadership. It was suggested that we establish a goal of complimenting (at least) one person for a job well done every day. It's a simple to-do item that requires little effort and virtually no advance planning—only a dose of genuine sincerity. Moreover, it makes both the giver and the recipient feel great. It's a win-win all around, and we're presented with opportunities every day. But nothing happens unless and until we actually do it.

As a boy, I was fortunate to have parents who appreciated the value of scouting. From the time I joined as a Cub Scout at the age of seven to the time I earned my Eagle Scout a decade later, they encouraged and supported me. Scouting taught me responsibility, duty, and a sense of obligation to serve my community. (In fact, I'm so appreciative of the lessons learned that I still include my Eagle Scout rank in my bio.)

The Boy Scouts also taught me respect—respect for myself and respect for others. Respect is the essence of the Golden Rule, and it's reflected in the Boy Scout Oath. Today, I may well forget my own phone number, but I haven't forgotten the Scout Oath. I can still recite it word-for-word and without hesitation.

> On my honor I will do my best
> To do my duty to God and my country
> and to obey the Scout Law;
> To help other people at all times;
> To keep myself physically strong,
> mentally awake, and morally straight.

Whereas the Scout Oath is a list of promises, the Scout Law is a twelve-word description of the ideal life we want to live. It's the equivalent of a vision statement as discussed in chapter three. It describes what every good scout strives to become and it reads as follows:

> A Scout is trustworthy, loyal, helpful, friendly,
> courteous, kind, obedient, cheerful, thrifty,
> brave, clean, and reverent.

These two pledges are worthy ingredients for any good life plan. Moreover, they're relevant and appropriate for men and women of all ages.

In chapter three, I referenced Jack, a successful business consultant who introduced me to the concept of "becoming." Besides being a businessman, Jack was a loving husband, a great father, and a dear friend. Unfortunately, he died unexpectedly way before his time. What happened at his funeral reconfirmed to all in attendance that Jack was indeed a good man who lived by the Golden Rule.

The funeral began as most do with hymns, readings, and reflections. As it drew to a close, however, the minister asked if anyone in the audience had anything they would like to add. After a long pause, an African-American man seated in the back of the church slowly rose to his feet. He wore neither a coat nor tie, and amidst the affluent white crowd he looked somewhat out of place.

"I do," he said before slipping into the aisle. Nervously, he made his way to the front of the church and approached the microphone. Eventually, he mustered the courage to speak, and a silenced crowd listened as the man told the story how he and Jack Jacobs become unlikely friends.

As it turned out, the man at the microphone ran a hot dog stand in downtown Austin, Texas, where Jack worked. One day Jack stopped by his stand and as he waited for his order, he noticed a photo of a fish taped to the stand.

"Do you like to fish?" Jack asked.

The man said he did. After a short conversation, Jack asked if he would like to go fishing at Jack's special place. The man accepted and, thereafter, the two men fished together many times. In fact, immediately prior to Jack's death, the two men had agreed to meet for yet another day of fishing. Only, when the date arrived, Jack didn't show.

"Jack was my friend," he said. "That's what he called me, and that's how he introduced me to others—as his friend. And I have never in my life really had anyone who was, or called me that: a friend."

We would all do well to follow Jack's example and live the Golden Rule.

Takeaway:

The Golden Rule is a simple but powerful personal oath. We would all do well to embrace and live it.

CHAPTER ELEVEN
Useful Tools of Do

"Persistence and determination alone are omnipotent."
— Calvin Coolidge

Until now, we've extolled the virtues of living a life of *do*, we've proposed methodologies for prioritizing pursuits, and we've discussed the scope of our obligations as doers. Yet, unless we can muster the motivation each day to take action, we will inevitably drift back into old habits. That's why it's important—particularly in the early going—to explore and consider all means, tools, and (even) tricks at our avail to keep us motivated and moving forward. In this chapter, we'll explore some of those methods.

These tools and methods fall into two broad categories: First, there are physical (or at least digital) tools that help us organize our personal and business lives. They help us get stuff done effectively, on time, and in order of priority. Secondly, there are mental tools and techniques we can employ each day to give us that extra motivation.

PHYSICAL TOOLS

The simplest physical tool is the to-do list. We've all employed one at some point in life, and therefore, it doesn't require much of an explanation. The nice thing about to-do lists is that they're clear and unambiguous. They display what's been accomplished and what hasn't. Akin to a roadmap, they show us how far we've been and how far we have to go. Today, they can be created and maintained on desktops, laptops, tablets, and smartphones using any number of downloadable applications.

Although I use these digital devices for other purposes, I prefer to manage my to-do list the Flintstone way—that is, using pen and paper. More specifically, I use a note card. Over the years, I've developed a habit of waking up each morning and writing down all of the to-do items for the coming day on a card. My lists are comprehensive and include both personal and business-related items. Once written, I then give each a priority rating of one, two, or three as follows:

Rating 1. Very important and due today.

Rating 2. Moderately important with a due date within the week. I do these if I have the time.

Rating 3. Least important to do today. These items are important but not urgent.

The ratings force me to prioritize my pursuits. When doing it, I use the same prioritization criteria used in the Do Wedge©: importance, urgency, and passion. As previously discussed, items shouldn't make it to our to-do lists unless we've vetted them first. As Steven Covey put it, "The key is not to prioritize what's on your schedule, but to schedule your priorities."

Though I'm partial, there are other advantages of maintaining your to-do list on cards or paper. First, items are easy to add and easy to scratch off. Second, I frequently tape mine to my computer where it remains in my peripheral vision throughout the workday.

At the end of each day (or first thing the following morning), I transfer the items that weren't completed onto the next day's to-do list. Over time, "two's" and "three's" migrate to "one's" and I eventually become annoyed with having to transfer them over- and-over and I get them done. Then, I get the satisfaction of scratching them off the list as completed.

On weekends I do the same thing, only I give myself a break with respect to prioritization. Though weekend items tend to be less urgent and sometimes less important, I still make my list on Saturday morning and hope to toss it in the trash by Sunday evening with each item completed.

Whether you choose to use an app on a device, note cards, or a sheet of paper, the point is to have a list and vigorously work it on a daily basis.

Speaking of technology, I actively use the calendar feature on my computer as well, and I refer to it constantly. Besides the normal appointments and meetings, I schedule exercise time and completion dates for specific to-do items as well as think time to plan for important projects. Throughout the day, dings remind me of events and to-do items.

Though they don't ding, "Flintstone" paper calendars can work as well as digital apps for some people. She won't appreciate the Stone Age reference, but my 85-year-old mother uses a paper calendar and doesn't miss a thing.

MENTAL TOOLS

Getting stuff done has much to do with our persistence, attitude, and determination (PAD). While organization and prioritization are critically important, they're no substitute for PAD. This is the softer mental side of being a doer and, as far as I know, there are no downloadable apps capable of generating PAD. We must develop these skills and traits on our own.

Some people seem to be born with more PAD than others. Even so, we choose for ourselves what we become. Determination, attitude, and persistence are all choices. I think of them as tools in a tool kit for life.

If our filtering and prioritization system (e.g., Do Wedge©) tells us what to do and in which order, it's our

PAD that converts it into reality. Figuratively speaking, the former is the nail and the latter is the hammer that drives it home. Without PAD, many of our aspirations—particularly those that are more difficult to achieve—just won't get done for all the reasons discussed in the previous chapter.

For years, two little plaques have hung on my office wall. They're my daily reminders of the power of PAD. One is a quote from Calvin Coolidge called "Press ON," which speaks to the power of persistence and determination. It reads:

Press ON

Nothing in the world can take the place of persistence. Talent will not; nothing is more common than unsuccessful men with talent. Genius will not; unrewarded genius is almost a proverb. Education will not; the world is full of educated derelicts. Persistence and determination alone are omnipotent.

Persistence and determination are often the difference between success and failure. The good news is that each of us can access and develop these qualities regardless of our

God-given brain circuitry. They can be critically important when we're drudging through tasks for which we have no burning passion. A good example for me would be fundraising.

Often I'm asked to help raise money for community projects. Because we intermittently raise money from investors, fundraising is a part of my day job as well. It's grinding work, and it takes all of the extra juice I can muster to do it consistently and well. But for my persistence, attitude, and determination, I would be inclined, at times, to toss my hands up and walk away.

Fundraising requires something else of me as well. I call it "professional persistence," and it's critically important to anyone pursuing a life of *do*. I think of professional persistence as a kind of audacity—a good kind of audacity.

While the word "audacity" conjures images of self-absorbed people doing what self-absorbed people do, this kind of audacity is different. If our dreams are big enough, we must be audacious in our thinking and actions to get things done. In this context, it's synonymous with extraordinary boldness, courage, and *chutzpah*.

The other plaque that adorns my office wall features a quote from Charles R. Swindoll:

> The longer I live, the more I realize the impact of attitude on life. Attitude, to me, is more important than facts. It is more important than the past, the education, the money, than circumstances, than failure, than successes, than what other people think or say or do. It is more important than appearance, giftedness or skill. It will make or break a company ...a church ...a home. The remarkable thing is we have a choice every day regarding the attitude we will embrace for that day. We cannot change our past ...we cannot change the fact that people will act in a certain way. We cannot change the inevitable. The only thing we can do is play on the one string we have, and that is our attitude. I'm convinced that life is 10% what happens to me and 90% of how I react to it. And so it is with you ...we are in charge of our attitudes.

In the life of a doer, attitude is all-important. A positive attitude—one that assumes the best as opposed to the worst in other people—drives the way we perceive and react to the world around us. A close cousin to a positive attitude is a can-do attitude—if you believe it, you can do it. Together, they are omnipotent.

As we awaken each morning, we choose the attitude we'll take with us into the day. It's no different than the way we choose the tasks we'll pursue or the level of persistence and determination we'll employ. We choose who we are and what we become.

With little more going for them than a positive attitude, people have overcome staggering odds in business and in life. The right attitude can lead us from despair to happiness. Positive attitudes have been known to cure diseases. In fact, attitude may be the single most powerful tool available in the box when it comes to succeeding in life. Most importantly, attitude is free, and only you can decide what yours will be.

The final tool in our box of tricks is called visualization. It's a technique of imagining a particular reality in order to make it so, and its origins go back for centuries. Today the best athletes in the world use it all of the time.

Over the years, I've emphasized the power of visualization by referencing (of all things) the North Carolina state motto, *Esse Quam Videri*, which means, "To be rather than to seem." Certainly, *being* a doer is better than *pretending* to be one. However, visualizing yourself as a disciplined doer in order to become one is not only acceptable, it's highly recommended.

As Buddha put it, "The mind is everything. What you think you become." I put it a little differently, "Think like a doer, and you'll become one."

Takeaway:

Fill your *do* box with the tools that work best for you, but leave plenty of room for persistence, attitude, determination, and (the good kind of) audacity.

CHAPTER TWELVE

Do What You Say You'll Do

"You are what you do, not what you say you'll do."
— C. G. Jung

The best employees, co-workers, bosses, friends, and volunteers are those who deliver on their commitments. Despite the size of the undertaking—from seemingly insignificant to momentous—once they say, "I'll do it," we know they'll deliver. Moreover they do it without having to be reminded, nudged, prompted, or cajoled.

Those who do what they say become the most successful

people in business and in life. They earn a reputation for dependability, which is often the difference between being an employee and an indispensible team member; a friend and a great friend; or a volunteer and an invaluable community leader. New opportunities present themselves to these people at every corner.

It's easy to make commitments. The opportunities are endless and constant. Whether motivated by a sense of obligation or a desire to please those around us, however, we often have a tendency to make commitments on the spur of the moment with little forethought.

"No problem, I'll handle it." "Sure, I'll give him a call." "No, I don't mind doing it." Whatever language we use to obligate ourselves, words of committal can leap from our tongues almost involuntarily. More often than not, they're made in good faith. That is to say we do it with the initial intention (or perhaps hope) that we'll actually deliver. Nevertheless, too many of these commitments end up forgotten, ignored, or in a perpetual holding pattern. If we break our promises, contemporaries will certainly notice. Eventually, they'll stop asking but not before our reputations are recast and diminished.

Thinking before committing is the first step in becoming a person who does what he or she says. Onboarding an obligation before reasonably considering its priority (relative to other obligations and pursuits) is a recipe for frustration and disappointment—for everyone involved. The bigger the obligation, the more time you should take to evaluate the decision.

Except for day trading and Jeopardy, there's no prize for committing the quickest. Practice restraint in saying, "I'll do it unless and until you know you mean it and you're confident that you can deliver on the promise within the time given or implied.

Assuming the commitment is worth your time (importance, passion, and urgency), the next step is to write it down. Whether you type it into an iPad, laptop, or smartphone, or whether you handwrite it on paper, don't rely solely on your biological memory unless you're Marilu Henner.

Sometimes unforeseen problems or circumstances impede us from delivering on the commitments we've made. In other words, stuff happens. Whether it precludes or merely delays execution, our response should be the same:

promptly notify the affected party with as much notice as possible.

While our tendency in these situations is to avoid making the unpleasant call, resist it. If we make the call early, it's never as bad as we think it will be. Just as you've been told all your life, "The longer you wait, the worse it gets." Give the affected party (or parties) a heads up that you can't complete the commitment or that you can't complete it within the agreed time. If delivery is still an option, offer a new completion date.

Great companies build and foster a culture of keeping commitments. Their employees understand that when they make promises to team members, there's an expectation that the tasks will be completed without further reminders. Saying you'll do something then failing to follow through is far more disruptive than never having made a commitment at all.

If you commit yourself to becoming a person who delivers on-time every-time, you can expect to be asked to do lots more. It comes with the territory. Your phone will ring off the hook, and your inbox will be full of folk wanting what you can bring to their project, movement, or organization. That's a good thing.

When you do what you say, people take notice. That, in turn, creates opportunities to do things, lead things, and participate in key initiatives that can make a difference in your own life and in the lives of others. That's a recipe for success and deep fulfillment.

As flattering as it is to have others clamoring for your time and assistance, that doesn't (and shouldn't) obligate you to accept all comers. Otherwise, as discussed in chapter s even, we become overloaded which inevitably compromises our ability to deliver.

Takeaway:
Do what you say you'll do, and doors will open.

CHAPTER THIRTEEN

Yoda's Wisdom

"Do or do not, there is no try."
— Yoda from *Star Wars*

The biggest and most transformational pursuits in life involve uncertainty ... great uncertainty. Starting a family, changing careers, launching a new business, or even writing a book all begin with uncertainty and risk.

Once we've considered our options, weighed the risks, and decided to embark upon a given pursuit, there is no room for timidity—particularly when it comes to big-ticket pursuits. Either proceed with dogged determination to succeed, or spare yourself the trouble and refrain altogether.

In The Empire Strikes Back, the diminutive Yoda teaches Luke Skywalker the ways of the Jedi. In one scene, Luke's crashed X-wing fighter suddenly slips deeper into the soupy Dagobah Swamp. In response, Luke plaintively trudges into the water with little hope or expectation of actually saving it. "I'll give it a try," he quips.

"No! Try not!" Yoda cries in response. "Do or do not. There is no try."

To be sure, there is nothing wrong with trying. In fact, nothing would ever be accomplished without someone first trying. However, once we commit to a particular pursuit, we should pursue it with the conviction that it can be accomplished and with an unflinching determination to get it done. Any half-hearted pursuit for the mere sake of trying is useless.

If you've ever raised teenagers, you'll recognize the latter "check off the box" variety of trying. Give them a labor-intensive (but doable) task and a common response is, "Uhhhh. There's no way I can do that." But, eventually, they trudge off with slumped shoulders only to return later with a disappointing but not surprising report: "See there. I told you I couldn't do it!"

Of course, this defeatist form of trying isn't just a teenage phenomenon. Adults do it as well. When working for any company or in any group environment—whether as employees of a company, team members of a volunteer organization, or otherwise—we won't always agree with the directives we're given. It's inevitable. When this occurs, we can and should offer our constructive recommendations. But when our advice isn't heeded, we have a choice. We can execute half-heartedly to prove (through failure) that our recommended path was better. Alternatively, we can accept our role and execute the directive with dogged determination to succeed. The latter is the way of the Jedi.

Living a life of *do* doesn't mean we're immune to failure. If we try frequently enough, we're bound to experience defeat, and it will happen in spite of our most diligent analysis and our most dogged determination to succeed. It's inevitable, so be prepared. You can lose a few battles and still win the war.

Everything worth doing comes with uncertainty … with risk. If there's no risk, there's no return. Whereas this concept is well understood in the investment world, it's equally applicable to life. If, for example, you took all of your retirement savings and locked it away in the most secure safe deposit box in the most secure vault in the most secure bank, your risk (as most people would define it) would be *de minimis*. But your return on that deposit would be zero ... nada. (Actually, because of inflation the real return would be negative, but you get the point.)

Likewise, if we close ourselves off from the world and make no effort to *do*, we can minimize our risk of being hurt; we can minimize our risk of financial loss; and we can minimize our risk of personal failure. Meanwhile, life passes us by. Tick ... tick ... tick.

We must take risk in order to experience a return, and if we invest long enough, we're going to experience losses—in life just as we do with investments. That's the deal.

So, when we experience defeat, what then?

Yoda, in his infinite wisdom, would advise us to prepare for these losses even before they happen. As he said in *Revenge of the Sith*, "Train yourself to let go of everything you fear to lose."

Our confidence, self-worth and sense of being can't hinge on our possessions. Possessions are fleeting. If we allow the size of our investment account to define us, then our worth rises and falls with the market. Should some unforeseen financial catastrophe befall us and our investments disappear, then our worth as a person quickly follows.

If we allow a relationship—whether with a friend, spouse, partner, or child—to define us, then we disappear if that relationship ends. If we're not careful, we'll set ourselves up to do *anything* to keep these possessions and relationships. That's not healthy.

As our friend Yoda put it, "The fear of loss is a path to the Dark Side." (And who could disagree with an 800-year-old Jedi Master?)

Losing is never pleasant, but with a healthy perspective, it doesn't have to be devastating. In fact, failures are invaluable life experiences. If we carefully and honestly examine our failures, we can always discover mistakes made or things we could have done differently. This can help us achieve a better outcome next go-round.

Most of the time, mistakes are precipitated by bad information and incorrect assumptions. Traced back, these are usually present at the outset, when the decision to pursue the opportunity was initially made. The key is to learn from our mistakes, and employ what we learn in future decisions.

Sometimes, however, failures are precipitated by actions or circumstances that are completely beyond our control. Not even the smartest economists, for example, anticipated the depth of the housing crisis that caused the Great Recession. In these situations we should look back and analyze (as best we can) why we didn't anticipate the condition that developed, but sometimes there's nothing we could have done differently.

We don't know everything, nor can we know everything. Consequently, some things just can't be predicted, forecasted, or anticipated. *We don't know what we don't know.* Often, these zingers appear as unexpected negative surprises like the Great Recession or the emergence of some disruptive new technology that adversely affects an existing industry. But there can also be good surprises. That's what makes life fun and exciting.

Whether good or bad, unexpected things are going to happen. All we can do in preparation is to live open and unafraid. Enjoy and capitalize on the good zingers, but be ready to step up and respond to the bad ones.

Finally, failures can also be attributable to faulty

execution. Execute is a synonym for *do*. In execution mode, as in *do* mode, we can only do the best we can while employing the best way we know how. We can carefully plan each step in a new pursuit, execute with all the determination we can muster, and make thoughtful mid-course corrections. Yet, in spite of our best efforts we'll still come up short. When this occurs (and it will) learn to dust yourself off and move on.

Helen Keller could neither see nor hear. But she had the wisdom to say, "Life is a succession of lessons which must be lived to be understood."

Takeaway:

**If at first you don't succeed, do do again.
If you still come up short, learn from it then move on.**

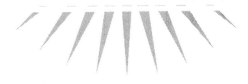

CHAPTER FOURTEEN

Living On

"Our passions and dreams live on."
— The Author

While on vacation a few years back, I heard a song by Van Morrison called "Rave On." As a Morrison fan, I had heard it before, but this time was different. One line in particular—"Rave on through the writing of a vision"—caught my attention and so stimulated my imagination that I did something I wouldn't normally do: I wrote a poem.

I equated the lyrics "rave on" with "living on," as in living inspired to do. I envisioned a switch, an "inspiration switch" so-to-speak, flipped to a perpetual "on" position. Later, with a pen and paper in hand, I sat in my hotel room and wrote the following lines that contrast a life of living inspired against a life of living uninspired—a life on versus a life off:

Living ON

Living ON beats living OFF
ON compels us to go and do
ON lights a path
ON looks ahead and bridges us to next
ON is productive
ON makes a difference
ON is accessible to all

ON is quick, and now, and doesn't wait
ON feels good but isn't easy
ON is a choice made every day
ON is viral
ON must rest to be its best, but
ON is active even in sleep

ON connects person to team

ON is collaborative

ON commits and sweats and endures

ON presses on, because

ON is driven to do

Our passions and dreams live ON

So live life ON

And rave ON about all who do

While marching ahead living ON

When we're living on, we can't hide it—nor should we. In this sense, it's analogous to the city on the hill as described in the book of Matthew (Chapter 5:13–20). It reads:

> You are the light of the world. A city built on a hill cannot be hid. No one after lighting up a lamp puts it under a bushel basket, but on the lamp stand, and it gives light to all in the house. In the same way, let your light shine before others, so they may see your good works and give glory to your Father in heaven.

Takeaway:

Live *on* and inspire others to do the same.

CHAPTER FIFTEEN

Do Can Be You!

"The privilege of a lifetime is to become who you truly are."

— C. G. Jung

Being authentic and true to one's self is a source of great power. As you embark upon a life of do, take care to ensure that the pursuits you choose align with and reflect your true and unique nature. Rather than adopt someone else's dream or follow someone else's path, pursue your own.

This concept—discovering and being true to one's own nature —is beautifully presented in a book by Bill George called True North. Though George's book is principally focused on leadership, his message applies to anyone pursuing a life of do. He describes five key dimensions to an authentic leader as follows:

- They pursue their chosen purpose with passion

- They practice solid values.

- They establish enduring relationships.

- They lead with their heart.

- They demonstrate self-discipline.

The life of a doer requires thought, energy, and courage, but the benefits are enormous. They extend beyond ourselves to affect our families, friends, and communities. This system, if you will, is graphically depicted in Figure 3.

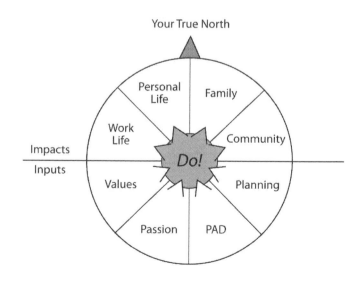

At the center of the circle is *do*. Think of it as you, the doer. From below, we feed, shape, and direct our doing nature with our own unique values, passions, and PAD (persistence, attitude, and determination) along with whatever prioritization tool we choose to employ. These are our inputs and efforts —the things that influence our pursuits, shape our approach, and determine our effectiveness.

The upper descriptors depict the benefits and beneficiaries of our *do* activities. These are the different lives we can and will affect as doers—including our personal lives, business lives, families, friends, and broader communities.

As you ponder what you've read, don't overcomplicate it. You have everything you need to become a doer, and you're closer than ever to flipping the switch. While *doing* does take a little planning, don't obsess over it. Planning isn't the desired end. It's the means to a desired end. The purpose of planning is to help you identify who you want to become and help you clear enough clutter so you can get there.

Hoping, wishing, and procrastinating without action are road signs to a less fulfilling life. The good news is that it's never too late to change direction. It's up to us to become who and what we want to be—to live a life of success and purpose.

Let's get doing!

Appendix

My hope is that after reading this book, you'll keep it handy and refer to it often. If nothing else, I hope it serves as a reminder to appreciate and live each day to the absolute fullest. The subtitles on the cover of the book are true. "By doing you become. Act on your passions and goals for a life of success and purpose."

Key summary points:

☑ Do is our choice.

☑ Do it now.

☑ Do for yourself.

☑ Do for others.

☑ *Do* is in all of us.

☑ *Do* = a life well-lived.

Takeaways from each Chapter:

☑ Do what matters ... NOW!

☑ What to do is informed by doing the analysis of what is important, urgent, and moves us to do.

☑ We can create the life we desire, if we plan and then do.

☑ The mind and body are mutually dependent. Exercise and maintain them both.

☑ Businesses can be instruments of good, and each of us has the ability to influence and leverage this potential.

☑ Our deepest level of satisfaction and highest sense of accomplishment come from doing for our communities.

☑ Overdoing can lead to diminished effectiveness and negative health consequences. Don't do it.

☑ Action requires courage, something we all have within us. Find it. Then do what you can to change the world.

☑ Fear and time can be impediments to do, but both can be overcome with a little planning and courage.

☑ The Golden Rule is a simple but powerful personal oath. We would all do well to embrace and live it.

☑ Fill your do box with the tools that work best for you, but leave plenty of room for persistence, attitude, determination, and (the good kind of) audacity.

☑ Do what you say you'll do, and doors will open.

☑ If at first you don't succeed, do do again. If you still come up short, learn from it then move on.

☑ Live on and inspire others to do the same.

☑ Let's get doing!

About the Author

Kel Landis, III, was born and raised in Rocky Mount, North Carolina, where at the age of 15 he earned his Eagle Scout. He attended the University of North Carolina-Chapel Hill wherehe earned a bachelor's degree in business and a master's degree in business administration.

Kel has over 30 years of experience in banking, financial services, investment management, and private capital and is a founding partner of Plexus Capital, a North Carolina—based investment firm. He co-founded Plexus Capital after retiringas CEO of RBC Centura Bank. Kel also serves as a director of Live Oak Bank, one of the leading lenders to small businessesacross the country.

Kel has served as a trustee of UNC-Chapel Hill, chair of the UNC Board of Visitors, trustee of Elizabeth City State University, and adjunct professor of finance for the Kenan- Flagler Business School. Currently, he is a member of the UNC Foundation's board of directors, a member of the board of visitors for the Kenan-Flagler Business School, and a trustee for the Kenan Institute for

Private Enterprise. Kel is also a William C. Friday Fellow for Human Relations.

Kel is the former chair of the North Carolina Bankers Association. He co-founded and served as chair of the Foundation of Renewal of Eastern North Carolina. In addition, he is a former board member for the Golden Leaf Foundation, a non-profit organization that supports grants for economically distressed communities. He also served as senior advisor for Business and Economic Affairs for the governor of North Carolina and as trustee of the North Carolina State Supplemental Retirement Fund. Today, Kel is a board member for the North Carolina Community Foundation, which provides support for community foundations across the state.

Earlier in his career, Kel was president of the Rocky Mount Chamber of Commerce, president of the Rocky Mount Area United Way, and president of the Rocky Mount Family YMCA. He was also treasurer of the local homeless shelter, a board member for Nash HealthCare Systems, and a board member for the North Carolina Citizens for Business and Industry. He is also a former member of the Young Presidents Organization.

For additional information, support, and inspiration go to:

www.littlebookofdo.com